Paddlewheelers of Alaska and the Yukon

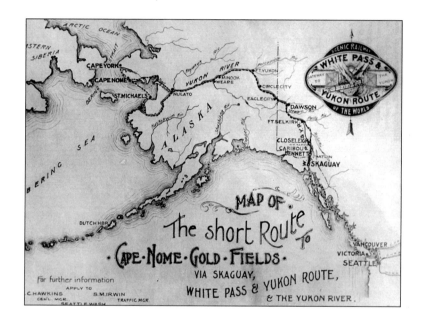

Graham Wilson

Research by
    Shawna McLarnon
Digital Pre-Press by
    Joel Edgecombe
Edited by Clélie Rich,
    Rich Words Editing
    Services, Vancouver, BC
Design and Production by
    Wolf Creek Books Inc.
Printed and Bound in
    Canada

Canadian Cataloguing in Publication Data

Wilson, Graham 1962-
Paddlewheelers of Alaska
and the Yukon

Includes index.
ISBN 0-9681955-5-5

1. Paddle steamers--Yukon
River (Yukon and Alaska)--
History--Pictorial works.
I. Title. II. Series
HE566.P3W54 1998
386'.22436
C98-900380-9

Acknowledgements

This book is the result of
the skill and support of
many people. Shawna
McLarnon provided
valuable detailed text
research. Joel Edgecombe
used digital pre-press tools
to enhance the quality of
images that were, in some
cases, more than a hundred
years old. John Small
streamlined the production
process and accessed
resources required for this
publication. Clélie Rich was
a joy to work with and
provided thoughtful and
meticulous editing. Finally,
Lauren Crooks and Emily
and Jessica Wilson were
supportive and made this
project possible.

WOLF CREEK BOOKS INC

Box 31275,
211 Main Street,
Whitehorse, Yukon
Y1A 5P7
info@wolfcreek.ca
www.wolfcreek.ca

CONTENTS

4

EARLY DAYS ON THE YUKON RIVER

The Yukon River is more than two thousand miles in length and is the fifth largest river in North America. Its watershed is largely a boreal forest ecosystem with large stands of evergreens and deciduous trees such as aspen. Winters are cold with substantial amounts of snow. Summers tend to be warm and relatively dry. At its mouth, the Yukon River, sediment-laden and massive, empties in the Bering Sea.

Indians have lived along the Yukon River for many thousands of years. These peoples established sophisticated societies with unique languages, arts and cultures. The rich annual salmon run on the Yukon River formed the basis of their economy. They also hunted caribou, moose, sheep and goats as well as birds and freshwater fish. Wild berries were collected as were various herbs and vegetables.

The first contact with the native peoples of this region was made by missionaries, prospectors and traders. Trading posts were established by Russians and later by the Hudson's Bay Company and others. Following this contact, native peoples suffered a range of epidemics. Scarlet fever, measles, influenza, dysentery as well as other plagues decimated the Indians of this region. Western trade dislocated traditional trade patterns and economies, and modernization brought many challenges. Contact meant massive change for the diverse indigenous cultures of the Yukon River region.

Five Indian porters at the start of the Chilkoot Trail, Alaska. Without the assistance of Indian porters, many stampeders would not have reached the Yukon. ca. 1898.

The introduction of paddlewheelers further accelerated the process of change. Paddlewheelers had been in use across North America for more than 50 years before the "Wilder", the first steamboat on the Yukon River, was launched by the Russian-America Company in 1866. A few years later the Hudson's Bay Company and the Alaska Commercial Company also launched paddlewheelers. These ships kept to the lower Yukon River

and rarely ventured into the upper Yukon River, most of which is in Canada.

During this early period there were only a handful of paddlewheelers on the entire Yukon River. Mostly these vessels supported small communities and prospectors and encouraged trade throughout Alaska, the Yukon and northern British Columbia. Wood camps scattered along this stretch of the river provided fuel and employment.

The increased trade the paddlewheelers brought meant significant changes to a number of Indian cultures throughout the region. Not only did this trade dislocate traditional trade patterns, but the types of goods and services available brought modernization to a region which had been somewhat ignored by the rest of the world. The Klondike Gold Rush would accelerate this process, and the Yukon River watershed changed from obscurity to fame overnight.

Above and Opposite Top: Indians carved elaborate canoes from cedar trees. These canoes are pictured on the Taku River but similar canoes were also used on the Yukon River. The large sails were traditionally made with moose hides and later with canvas. Indians also made skin boats and rafts for navigating northern rivers and lakes.

Opposite Bottom: A group of Indians standing behind a sled loaded with trade goods on Front Street, Dawson City. ca. 1898.

BONANZA!

When the small steamship *Excelsior* docked in San Francisco in July 1897, the world was watching. Aboard this vessel were millionaires who had been penniless men only months before. As these scruffy miners swaggered down the gangplank carrying jars, satchels and cases filled with gold, more than five thousand people crowded the docks and cheered. A few days later the steamship *Portland* landed at Seattle with sixty-eight miners and almost a ton of gold. The news of the find grabbed newspaper headlines and was on everyone's lips.

Within days thousands flocked to west coast towns from San Francisco to Vancouver trying to book passage north. The fact that the Klondike was more than fifteen hundred miles away and over a precipitous mountain pass would not deter many. Gold fever had grasped the nation, and everyone wanted the chance to try their luck in the new frontier.

The wealthy booked passage on steamships to the port of St. Michael, at the mouth of the Yukon River on the Bering Sea. Paddlewheel steamships then carried them up the Yukon River to Dawson City.

Less well-heeled stampeders faced one of the most arduous treks imaginable. They traveled up the coast in overcrowded and often decrepit ships. They spent the winter ferrying supplies over the cold and dangerous Chilkoot and White Passes, then built rickety boats and navigated the lakes and rapids of the Yukon River.

Whatever their route, most stampeders arrived in Dawson in the spring and summer of 1898. Dawson City had a population of more than 40,000. In its heyday Dawson was the largest city west of Winnipeg and north of San Francisco.

Steamship "City of Seattle" in Glacier Bay, Alaska, with Muir Glacier in the background.

For a short time Dawson was the "Paris of the North" and had a range of goods and services that haven't been seen since. In Dawson you could buy the best champagne and sip it in the finest crystal. You could dine on filet mignon, oysters and caviar. Fine silks, jewelry and

gowns were available for a price. Virtually anything was possible in Dawson. Paddlewheelers bound for Dawson were loaded to capacity not only with stampeders, but also luxuries and essentials.

Entrepreneurs took note of the difficulties involved in reaching the gold fields. Soon paddlewheelers were being brought to the Yukon River from across the Pacific Northwest. By the summer of 1898 there were more than 110 paddlewheelers on the lower Yukon River alone. This number would more than double during the next couple of years. The rush was on.

The irony of the Klondike Gold Rush was that the gold fields had been almost entirely staked the year before the stampeders arrived. There was little opportunity for day laborers and many stampeders were flat broke. By the autumn of 1899, Dawson was relatively deserted. The vast majority of the stampeders left the Yukon without making a cent.

Above: Stampeders amid mountains of supplies landed near the mouth of the Taiya River, near Dyea.

Opposite: Stampeders ascending the "Golden Stair" portion of the Chilkoot Trail.

On Chilkoot Pass

Above: Stampeders navigating the treacherous rapids of Miles Canyon on the Yukon River.

Opposite Top: Interior view of a log cabin near Dawson City. Stampeders are drying their clothing next to a wood stove.

Opposite Bottom: A tent store specializing in fresh lemonade. Stores such as this could earn their proprietors a small fortune.

Pages 14 and 15: A small paddlewheeler towing several barges on Bennett Lake. The tent town of Bennett can be seen in the background. September 1899.

94. LEAVING BENNETT FOR DAWSON

'99.

H.C.BARLEY.

THE RICH MAN'S ROUTE TO DAWSON

With the increased demand for paddlewheelers, the community of St. Michael flourished. This former Russian trading post became a boom town overnight. St. Michael was a break-of-bulk point where ships dropped supplies and passengers for paddlewheelers to take them to Dawson City. Warehouses, restaurants, hotels and a variety of businesses instantly emerged. This town also had a thriving shipyard which assembled paddlewheelers sent as freight from Victoria, Portland and Seattle.

In 1900, a first class ticket from St. Michael to Dawson City could cost more than $100. Initially there were more passengers than berths on the paddlewheelers, and the free market prevailed as ticket prices jumped in value. The distance from St. Michael to Dawson City is more than two thousand miles. This journey usually took more than a month. As comparatively comfortable as this route to the Klondike was, it was a great distance to travel. Passengers spent their days lounging on deck or in simple parlors. Meals could be elegant for first class passengers and more simple for coach and crew. First class berths were usually located on the upper deck and were provided with scenic views, heat and, in some cases, bathrooms.

An entertainer popular in Dawson City during the Gold Rush.

By 1900, however, the White Pass and Yukon Route Railway was in operation making it possible to travel from Skagway to Whitehorse by rail. Paddlewheelers at Whitehorse could bring people to Dawson City within a few days, making a trip from Seattle to Dawson City easily possible within a couple of weeks. Unassembled paddlewheelers could also be sent by rail from Skagway to Whitehorse. The community of St. Michael began to falter.

STEAMBOAT ROW,

ST MICHAEL, JULY 28, 1899.

Opposite and Above: The beaches of St. Michael were littered with paddlewheelers and construction materials. Most paddlewheelers were built elsewhere and brought to Alaska by ship. They were assembled at St. Michael and prepared for the long journey up the Yukon River. St. Michael was a boom town which thrived during the Klondike Gold Rush as a shipyard and as a break-of-bulk point for supplies being shipped inland.

The rush from the head of navigation has only about one-half arrived, yet the rush for the lower river is in full swing, and more people are leaving daily than arriving. The place of wealth—where you don't have to work for it, but just pick it up—is always just beyond, and the crowd always follows the butterfly. Those who remain and honestly go to work at something, will make a stake, great or small, if they will only exercise such economy and precaution as they would in any other part of the country.
Klondike Nugget, 23 June 1898

The beaches (of St. Michael, Alaska) are another great
curiosity. They are crowded with camps of parties preparing to
go with the Yukon, engaged most of them in constructing
wonderful river craft.
George R. Putnam

*Above: A card party in progress
while the "Rock Island" steams its
way to Dawson City. ca. 1898.*

Above: A woman standing on the upper deck of a paddlewheeler on the Whitehorse-Dawson City run as it passes four sternwheelers up on skids at Lower Laberge.

Pages 22 and 23: A group of people dancing on the deck of the "Scotia." Passengers commonly entertained themselves with games, dances and concerts.

The next stop was old Circle City, a gold mining region of yore.
Where wood was put on for the furnace, and freight was put on for the store.
Then, on to the village of Eagle. Then, Forty Mile Station was passed:
And, puffing, and chunking, and chugging, the steamer reached Dawson at last.
John H. Kelly, "The Log of the Yukon"

Opposite: The "White Horse" laden with passengers leaving Dawson City.

Above: A.E. Company paddlewheeler "Arnold" leaving Dawson City on her first trip to St. Michael in 1899. The decks of the ship are crowded with passengers.

As a depot and port of trans-shipment it (St. Michael) seems destined to flourish as the Suez of the northern seas.
Alaska and the Gold Fields of the Yukon, Koyukuk, Tanana, 1898

The greatest sight is the shipping in the harbor (St. Michael, Alaska)—there are from forty to fifty vessels here of all natures and descriptions, from the large liners brought from the Atlantic and Europe, down to the most remarkable freaks of river boats. Fifteen boats and barges have arrived here today, most of them for the river trade. Klondikers are returning with their gold.
George R. Putnam, 1898

Above: The dining rooms on some paddlewheelers were elegant and formal.

Above: Passengers patiently wait to be seated for dinner. Meals could be very elaborate on paddlewheelers. It was not uncommon for the fanciest foods available anywhere in the world to be served and washed down with champagne.

We started eating on our boat yesterday morning and man, how do I eat! We have the best cooks this year we have had since I have been up here. Tonight's menu, besides three kinds of meat and the vegetables that go with them, had pumpkin pie, peach pudding, cherry tarts and chocolate cake cut in three inch slices. How can I keep my waistline down that way?
Art Knutson, former mate for the British Yukon Navigation Company

THE PERFECT CRAFT

In many ways the paddlewheeler was the perfect craft to navigate the Yukon River. These ships were carefully designed and adapted to the often harsh northern conditions. Paddlewheeler designs varied widely depending on the cargo they were intended to carry, the nature of the river and the fashions of the day when they were built. The goal was to build a hull which could support the greatest weight on the shallowest draft while allowing for speed and maneuverability. The paddlewheelers of the Yukon were built with the sand and gravel bars of the Yukon River in mind and tended to have a shallow draft, with a long, wide, flat hull and no keel.

To provide stability and to prevent the hull from sagging, "hog chains" were attached from the bow to the stern. This stiffened the hull and allowed for adjustments depending on the weight of the load carried or the conditions of the river. Use of hog chains also meant that the paddlewheelers could be built with local wood of less hefty dimensions.

Paddlewheelers usually had a locomotive boiler system. Large steam-driven pistons drove the paddles and winches on the decks. On most ships wood fuel was stored below decks in relatively small amounts to keep the loaded weight of the ship to a minimum. As many ships consumed more than a cord of wood each hour, wood camps sprang up along the river.

The superstructure of paddlewheelers provided staterooms and a wheelhouse. The height of the wheelhouse allowed crewmen better visibility to navigate the river. To prevent the ship from becoming top heavy, light woods were used at minimal dimensions.

Bow view of the paddlewheeler "Canadian."

First class passengers enjoyed luxurious accommodation and amenities. The staterooms had windows opening to the outside, and, in some cases, bathrooms. On early ships, stewards brought hot water to the rooms and prepared baths for patrons as well. On later ships, hot and cold water plumbing was provided. Later ships also had electric lights and heaters. Second class passengers

received less elaborate accommodation and usually slept on cots below decks. Paddlewheelers had dining rooms, observation rooms and other common areas. Masquerade parties, dances and concerts provided lively evening entertainment.

Above: The "Canadian" on the Yukon River near Dawson City. ca. 1926.

Paddlewheelers operated in the days before radar when crewmen had to rely on experience and simple charts to navigate the ever-changing river. At night a large electric light illuminated the river so that ships could travel around the clock. Crew members over the years nailed hundreds of metal pie plates to trees along the river to act as reflectors and aid night navigation. Prior to the introduction of the radio in 1925, the only means of communication in an emergency was to hook a portable phone to the telegraph line which followed the river. These adaptations and innovations allowed a reliable and relatively safe and comfortable means of transportation to be developed.

Above: The "Bailey" was considered an average size paddlewheeler. This ship had an extremely active career and logged thousands of miles of service on the Yukon River.

Pages 32 and 33: The "Tyrrell" on the Whitehorse to Dawson City run. ca. 1900.

You may romance all you choose about steamboating but it would be very difficult to convince a deckhand, pilot, mate or engineer of a boat stuck on a sandbar with the water level dropping because the tributaries were freezing, that there was anything good to be said about that damn way to make a living.

Art Knutson, former mate for the British Yukon Navigation Company

Opposite Top: The "D.R. Campbell" docked at Dawson City along with the "Seattle No. 1," "Leon" and the "Otter." ca. 1900.

Opposite Bottom: On June 21, 1898 the "A.J. Goddard" was the first paddlewheeler on the upper Yukon River to reach Dawson City. It is pictured next to two unidentified paddlewheelers. ca. 1898.

Above: Partial view of the "Arnold" docked at Dawson City with the "Mary F. Graff" alongside. ca. 1899.

Above: The "Australian" docked along with the "William Ogilvie" and the "Nora" at Canyon City. This site is upstream of the treacherous Miles Canyon rapids on the Yukon River. ca. 1899.

Opposite Top: A large crowd gathered on the docks and on the deck of the "Monarch" at her arrival in Dawson City on July 21, 1898. The tent town of West Dawson is visible in the background.

Opposite Bottom: View from the Yukon River looking east towards Dawson City. The "Canadian" is docked at the Canadian Development Company dock.

Pages 38 and 39: The "Casca" and the "Whitehorse" docked side-by-side, probably at Dawson. ca. 1920.

The North American Transportation and Trading Company...
has developed this route and has now improved its
transportation facilities to the point, that even delicate women
who desire to take a brief glimpse of the wonderful life of a
new and uncommonly rich mining camp, can make a summer
excursion to the Klondyke and return, all the time enjoying all
the comforts which can be had on any steamer.
Gold Fields of Alaska, 1898

Above: The "Columbian" along
with the "Canadian" at Dawson
City. It was common for crowds to
gather when paddlewheelers
arrived. ca. 1899.

Above: The "Bonanza King" laden with passengers on its first excursion to Forty Mile, north of Dawson City. May 28, 1899.

It was a royal reception that the steamer A.J. Goddard received as she made her landing at the foot of Fourth Street Tuesday afternoon. The vessel was in charge of A.J. Goddard, head of the Upper Yukon Company, and made the run from the head of Lake Bennett to this city (Dawson City) in four days and 21 hours.
Klondike Nugget, 23 June 1898

Above: The "Gleaner" and "Australian" at dock at the head of Miles Canyon. At this point supplies were loaded onto flat cars of the Whitehorse Tram Line. ca. 1899.

Opposite Top: The "Bella" pushing a barge leaving Dawson City. ca. 1898.

Opposite Bottom: The Dawson waterfront was littered with ships, supplies, and waste.

Pages 44 and 45: The "Whitehorse" winching upstream through Five Finger Rapids. The crew on the deck worked the cable around the steam-driven winch on the front deck.

Opposite Top: The "Governor Pingree" of Seattle underway near Dawson City. This paddlewheeler was later renamed the "Bonanza King" of the Flyer Line. ca. 1898.

Opposite Bottom: Celebrations were common in Dawson City. The "Governor Pingree" and "Philip P. Low" are docked. Front Street businesses, warehouses and various small boats are also visible. ca. 1898.

Above: A paddlewheeler navigates the broad Yukon River. ca. 1900.

It was nearly five when several who were on the lookout for the first sight of steamboats saw a puff of smoke arising far up the bend beyond Klondike City. The cry of "Steamboat" was raised and the ubiquitous street gamins took it up and half the houses of the city emptied themselves, everyone rushing down to the waterfront to greet the craft so welcome. Seemingly within five minutes every dock was black with people and as the first boat appeared and tooted a merry good evening there was a yelling and cheering loud enough to awaken the dead.

The Klondike Nugget, May 1902

WOOD CAMPS

Virtually all paddlewheelers were fueled with wood. In the north, oil would have had to be imported and could have led to many supply complications if used as fuel. Wood could be supplied locally and meant that ships did not have to carry a lot of fuel.

Trees were cut by hand with axe and saw during the winter and dragged by horse-driven sleighs to a central woodlot next to the river. Wood was cut into four-foot lengths and all branches were removed. When paddlewheelers landed to refuel, the wood was loaded onto large handcarts and driven down a long gangplank into the paddlewheeler. Most steamers consumed at least 120 cords of wood to make the round-trip journey from Whitehorse to Dawson City and back.

Cutting wood with simple tools was very labor intensive. Many locals, both native and non-native, were hired each winter. Wood camps provided jobs during a time of the year when unemployment was high. The practice of hiring natives was significant and for some led to careers working on the paddlewheelers. For most, however, the wood camps allowed them to bridge a traditional economy with the ability to make a wage. Many native woodcutters moved their entire family to the wood camp for the winter.

Wood camps were scattered up and down the Yukon River every fifty to hundred miles. When the forest was depleted, the wood camp would be moved to another location. Crews lived in tents or small cabins and lived under primitive conditions. The camps were located at parts of the river where the river bank was low, with a waterdepth suitable for a paddlewheeler to land. Sometimes ice jams and a rapid thaw caused the Yukon River to flood. In these cases, an entire season's work could be swept away in hours.

Stern view of the "Tutshi" docked at Engineer Mines along the shore of Taku Arm, Bennett Lake. The "Tutshi" was launched in 1917 and serviced a number of communities at the headwaters of the Yukon River. ca. 1924.

Above: The "W.K. Merwin" docked at Dawson City with passengers, crew and fuel wood on deck. ca. 1899.

Opposite Top: A crowd gathered to greet the "Canadian," the first paddlewheeler of the 1923 season to reach Mayo, Yukon. Ore sacks and some timber are strewn on the bank. May 18, 1923.

Opposite Bottom: The "Clifford Sifton" docked at Carcross, Yukon. ca. 1899.

CLIFFORD SIFTON

H.C.

Above: Four men watch the "Casca" leave Dawson City. ca.1926.

Opposite Top: Portrait of "Bucky" Buckholtz in an Alaska-Yukon Navigation Company uniform. ca.1920.

Opposite Bottom: A paddlewheeler unloading supplies. Laborers used large handcarts to empty the holds of paddlewheelers. This was strenuous work which employed many people.

The pace of shipboard life was a relaxed one for the passengers, which I appreciated after a season of laboring. We played shuffleboard, took afternoon naps, watched the crew taking on wood at our fuel stops, using two-wheeled baggage carts which were loaded by hand and which were wrestled up the gangplanks that were often quite steep—the White Pass obviously did not believe in labor-saving devices.
Art Knutson, former mate for the British Yukon Navigation Company

Above: Profile of the "Yukon" at the river shore. ca.1930.

Opposite Top: The "Whitehorse" docking at a wood camp. Passengers and crew on deck and a log cabin along the bank. There were only a handful of docks on the entire Yukon River and crews had to be skilled to land these ships without mishap.

Opposite Bottom: The "Bella" and a barge she is pushing loading fuel wood. The "Bella" is loaded with freight and supplies enroute from St. Michael to Dawson. July 1897.

"THE CHALLENGE"

THE RACE IS ON

Being the first paddlewheeler to reach Dawson City each spring was a coveted prize requiring endurance, the courage to navigate the partially frozen river and a lot of luck. Races from St. Michael to Dawson City were common and often included dozens of ships. Lookouts were stationed on high banks in Dawson City and would signal when the first paddlewheeler was in sight. The entire town would empty on to the docks and riverbank to cheer. The first ship of the season brought news from the "outside" world, staples, luxuries, and entertainers. It brought a festive, almost carnival atmosphere to a town isolated by a long winter.

Racing paddlewheelers had a long tradition in other regions such as the Mississippi. On the Yukon River it became part of the competitive spirit of the Klondike. Everyone was focused on being first, and fastest at whatever they did. After all, the Klondike was a "rush" in all sorts of ways.

During celebrations it was common for paddlewheelers to race upstream from Dawson City to Whitehorse. These races were carefully reported by local newspapers and were followed by many residents. The prize for the winner was often a case of wine or a coveted broom, which the winner displayed outside the wheelhouse at the front of the paddlewheeler.

Racing paddlewheelers displayed the confidence and skill of the ships' crews. Being able to navigate the river under full speed and trying to pass other ships while staying off sandbars and rocks was not for the faint-hearted. These ships raced around the clock for days on end and tested their crews' stamina and the ships' integrity. Sometimes ships crashed into one another or landed on rocks and were damaged.

The "Bailey" on the Fifty Mile River. In the foreground is the deck of the paddlewheeler she is racing. ca. August 1899.

With the decline in the gold rush and the monopoly of river transportation by the White Pass and Yukon Railway, racing became less common and eventually ceased all together. An era on the Yukon River was over.

Opposite Top and Bottom: The "Bailey" racing on the Fifty Mile section of the Yukon River. August 1899.

Above: The Canadian Development Company's "Columbian" and the Yukon Flyer Line Company's "Eldorado" in a Fourth of July race from Dawson City to Whitehorse. The race was shortened to the mouth of the Klondike River, only a short distance from Dawson City. July 1899.

THE WHITE PASS MONOPOLY

The completion in 1900 of the White Pass and Yukon Route Railway had broad implications for paddlewheelers on the Yukon River. Most significantly, the railway reduced the need to transport freight to St. Michael. Paddlewheelers at Whitehorse had only 400 miles to travel to Dawson City which meant that supplies could easily travel from Skagway to Dawson in under a week.

Bulk supplies could now be shipped relatively inexpensively and the return trip upriver could carry minerals such as gold, and later, silver ore. Paddlewheelers started to follow more rigid schedules which coincided with the train timetable and with steamships bringing passengers and cargo from the south.

Once the railway reached Whitehorse, most paddlewheelers at the headwaters of the Yukon River were out of work. Towns such as Bennett were deserted. Since there was no longer any need for most of the paddlewheelers on the upper reaches of the Yukon River watershed, they were lowered on steel cables through Miles Canyon to start service on the Whitehorse to Dawson City run.

The White Pass and Yukon Route Company vigorously pursued its paddlewheeler division called the British Yukon Navigation Company. Since it already owned the railway it had a competitive advantage by offering passengers and freight companies incentives to book their entire trip from Skagway to Dawson City. This reliable, albeit expensive, service was a contrast to the chaos of the Gold Rush era.

Bow view of the "Bailey" stopped to load wood on the Fifty Mile River. August 1899.

The combination of the railway with paddlewheelers brought goods and services never before available in the north and established a modern trade network. This network displaced the business of traders such as the Hudson's Bay Company which had established posts throughout the Yukon River watershed. The network also held great implications for northern native peoples.

As a result of the railway and the depopulation of the region following the Klondike Gold Rush, many small paddlewheeler companies collapsed while others struggled for the next decade. Paddlewheelers had become an unprofitable business during this period. Following the Klondike Gold Rush, paddlewheeler rate wars were common, with prices dropping from $26 to $5 for a regular ticket from Whitehorse to Dawson City. It was survival of the fittest.

In April 1914, the White Pass and Yukon Route Railway bought the rival Northern Navigation company and its 42 paddlewheelers. Since these ships were redundant, many were pulled out of the water and left to rot. By 1915, the White Pass and Yukon Route Company had a virtual trade monopoly on the upper Yukon River.

Whitehorse was founded as a transfer point between the rail and river. In the true sense of the word, Whitehorse was a company town with much of its land and employment in the control of the White Pass and Yukon Route Company. The few hundred residents either worked in the shipyards, railyards or in some other capacity for the White Pass and Yukon Route.

Paddlewheelers on the lower Yukon River were also experiencing tough times. The combination of the depopulation of the Klondike region after 1899 and the growth of the White Pass and Yukon Route Railway freight system led to the decline and abandonment of many small communities. Other communities were founded as "echo booms" followed the Klondike Gold Rush. Overnight, hundreds of stampeders would stake claims on little more than a rumor. Within months the town would collapse and only a fraction of its population would remain.

A train speeding across the timber trestle spanning Glacier Gorge. ca. June 1901

The establishment of the Alaska Railroad in 1922 pushed most of the remaining paddlewheel companies on the lower Yukon River out of business. The Alaska Railroad linked Valdez, Fairbanks and Nenana and with its river boats serviced a even larger region. This railroad was publicly owned and its rates were low and its service superior to that of previous companies.

Above: Passengers standing in front of a train parked under the hanging rock at Clifton. ca. 1901.

Opposite Top: A train stopped in the middle of the steel cantilever bridge spanning Dead Horse Gulch near the summit of the White Pass. Construction of the *bridge was completed in early 1901.*

Opposite Bottom: Members of the Senatorial Party in an open flatbed car.

Pages 66 and 67: A train stopped on the trestle bridge in front of a tunnel.

A little more than one year ago a company began what was then considered an impossible task, that of constructing a railroad from Skagway to the summit of White Pass. But where energy and money combine, defeat is unknown. Work was constantly carried on and never for one moment was there any flagging. Through a wild and rocky country where formerly the mountain goat dared not venture, a road bed was constructed, steel rails were laid over which thundered the iron horse drawing in his wake material for further construction....Yesterday the road was completed to Bennett, making it possible for travelers from any part of the United States to reach Dawson City on one continuous journey on rail and water where all the comforts of life may be enjoyed; no walking, no packing of outfits on backs of men and beasts, and with no delays.
The Daily Alaskan, July 1899

Above and Opposite: A large crowd gather to watch the "Golden Spike Ceremony" commemorating the completion of the railway to Bennett. The "Australian" and "Gleaner" are offshore. July 6, 1899.

Pages 70 and 71: The "Clifford Sifton" and "Bailey" loading supplies at Bennett. The White Pass and Yukon Route Railway delivered supplies to Bennett Lake. During the winter warehouses were stuffed to the rafters with supplies. After the spring break-up of Bennett Lake and the Yukon River paddlewheelers hurriedly emptied these warehouses. ca. 1899.

At White Horse we turned them over to an irresponsible mob of river steamers that competed for the business in much the same fashion as cab-drivers outside an ill-managed railway station. Innocent passengers were fought over, through shipments of goods were split up, customs papers lost, goods stolen on the boats, and in short perfect anarchy prevailed. Many of the boat owners were not responsible financially, so that the passengers with through tickets and the goods owners with through bills of landing naturally preferred to make their claims agains us, leaving us in turn to recover from the delinquent boat owners—if we could. Before the end of the season of 1900, it was obvious that in self-defense we must recognize our own river service.
S.H. Graves, White Pass and Yukon Route Manager, 1908

Above: The "Casca" and "Whitehorse" docked at Whitehorse. ca.1920.

Opposite Top: The British-Yukon Navigation Company fleet in the Whitehorse shipyards. ca.1901.

Opposite Bottom: The "Dawson" and "Whitehorse" under construction at the British-Yukon Navigation Company shipyard at Whitehorse. April 1901.

THE B.Y.N. FLEET LAID UP FOR THE WINTER OF 1901

We have completed the best possible facilities for handling perishables at Whitehorse...and are in a position to handle goods with the least possible delay, and greatest care. A wharf, the best on the river, 800 feet long, has been built, and on it a warehouse 40x60 feet, which will accommodate about 3,000 tons of freight. Three tracks are laid on the wharf and cars coming in loaded are run right down to the steamer's side, and the freight transferred direct from car to steamer, which arrangement possesses great advantages over the old way. E.C. Hawkins, General Manager of the White Pass and Yukon Route Railway, Daily Klondike News, 6 August 1900

Above: The "Dawson" docked at one of the wood camps on the Yukon River. A small tug or mail boat is docked alongside.

Opposite Top: The "Wilbur Crimmin" docked at Whitehorse near the White Pass and Yukon Route freight sheds. Four other paddlewheelers are dry-docked in the background. ca. 1901.

Opposite Bottom: White Pass and Yukon Route Railway paddlewheeler underway at Whitehorse. The "Dawson" is docked.

Above: The "Casca No. 3"
underway on the Yukon River
pushing a barge.

Opposite Top: The British-Yukon
Navigation paddlewheeler the
"Whitehorse" with workmen
posing on all decks having their
picture taken. The construction of
the "Whitehorse" was completed

43 days after the keels were laid in
the Whitehorse shipyard. In the
background are the "Dawson" and
the "Selkirk." May 25, 1901.

Opposite Bottom: The "Tutshi"
docked at Carcross, Yukon. The
"Tutshi" serviced Bennett and
Tagish Lakes and the upper
Yukon River.

Opposite Top: The "Alaska" underway pushing a loaded barge. ca. 1900.

Opposite Bottom: The "Casca No. 2" docked at Hootalinqua on the Yukon River.

Above: The "Scotia" underway on Atlin Lake, BC.

The arrival of the first steamer in the spring at the starved-out camps has been always hailed with the same delight as would a column coming to the relief of a beleaguered garrison. It was an event in which not only every miner was expected to turn out and take part by waving his hat and cheering, but as the deep whistle of the incoming boat was blown every Malamut dog lifted its voice in a doleful wail.
Tappan Adney, Journalist, 1899

THE FROZEN NORTH

Shipping on the Yukon River was hampered by ice and the long northern winter. By September most ships were busy transporting the last supplies of the season to communities and camps. Paddlewheelers were also busy carrying passengers leaving the north. During this time it was common for northern workers in a variety of professions to winter in the south. This migration was common and is a testament to the relative ease transportation had acquired. Navigation on the Yukon River usually ended in mid-October.

Freeze-up could happen suddenly and more than one paddlewheeler was trapped unexpectedly in the ice. These ships faced the prospect of being crushed by shifting ice in the spring break-up. Waiting in the middle of the frozen river until spring was intimidating, especially if there was a reasonable chance of having your ship splintered by drift ice.

Paddlewheelers were either parked in sloughs or lakes or were hauled out of the water for the winter. Sloughs provided protection from drifting ice and were considered a relatively safe moorage. The mouth of Lake Laberge is somewhat sheltered and was also a popular place to over-winter. Usually a caretaker was assigned to each ship to care for it all winter.

Paddlewheelers requiring work were hauled out at several places along the river. Hauling paddlewheelers out of the water required massive horse-driven, and later, motorized, capstans. Lines were secured along the ship and it was slowly dragged broadside along greased timbers from the riverbank to the shore. In the spring the process was reversed and the paddlewheeler slid into the river.

The "Prospector" arriving in Dawson City encrusted in ice and snow. The "Prospector" was the last paddlewheeler of the year to arrive from Whitehorse on October 20, 1903.

Paddlewheelers were remodeled, repaired and refurbished during the winter. The frenetic pace of the summer left little time to care for ships. The shipyards employed many and established some of the first modern manufacturing to be done in the north.

Above: People boarding the "Dawson" along the ice-covered shore of the Stewart River.

Opposite Top: The "Columbian," "Canadian," "Yukoner" and "Sybil" up on the skids at the Whitehorse drydock. ca.1901.

Opposite Bottom: The "Australian" under construction at Bennett (its superstructure is almost complete). The Canadian Development Company building is in the foreground. May 1899.

The ice carries everything before it—a ponderous battering ram that can be heard 15 miles away. During break-up the ice moves about 100 miles a day, crunching over or levering aside all obstacles. It was this battering ram that claimed three of the four pioneer vessels on the river.
Fergus Cronin

Above: A North West Mounted Police officer and his dog team in front of a paddlewheeler. ca.1895.

Above: "Malamute Bill" with his dog team in front of the "Yukoner" on the frozen Yukon River near Dawson. ca. March 1900.

Pages 86 and 87: Paddlewheelers wintering at the Dawson Slough across from Dawson City. The "Tyrrell" is the only paddlewheeler identifiable. ca. 1905-1906.

It grew steadily colder—no thermometer was needed to show that. Our own was a cheap affair of the familiar summer veranda style.... It kept shortening until it showed -50 degrees, but when it suddenly landed in the bulb at, at least, -65 degrees we threw the thing away.
Tappan Adney, Journalist, 1899

Above and Opposite: Horse-drawn sleighs in winter and horse-drawn coaches in the fall and spring traveled the 330 miles between Whitehorse and Dawson City. Road houses were scattered every 22 miles and provided simple meals and accommodation. The journey took about five days and provided an important link between communities.

Pages 90 and 91: Skaters on the Tanana River at Fairbanks.

Drawn by four splendid horses, this open sleigh is a very comfortable affair, being upholstered and roomy with plenty of good fur robes and provided with foot warmers.... Amid handshaking, good wishes and the hearty cheers of the bystanders, our jolly coachman cracks his long whip and off we start swiftly and silently over the pure white snow.
Selina Howard, 1910

The launching was a big success and the handsome craft, whose lines are as fine as an ocean greyhound, took to the water as gracefully and naturally as an aquatic bird.
The Weekly Star, commenting on the launching of the "Tutshi" in Carcross, 15 June 1917

Above: The Canadian Development Company paddlewheelers the "Canadian" and the "Lotta Talbot" in winter quarters at Whitehorse. ca. 1900.

Opposite Top: The "Gleaner" being launched broadside from timber skids at Carcross. ca. 1915.

Opposite Bottom: The "Alaska" being launched from timber skids in Whitehorse shipyards dry-dock. The "Bonanza King" is partially visible in background. ca. 1915.

SHIPS ARE LOST

Paddlewheeler crews were well trained and relatively highly paid professionals. Many captains had worked on other great rivers such as the Mississippi or had extensive sea experience. Senior crew members were also well trained and most ships had a complement of qualified skilled seamen. Untrained crew members were employed as simple laborers in positions like stewards, cleaners or below decks keeping the boilers stoked.

The Yukon River was a challenge for the most seasoned crew. Rocks, sandbars and snags could appear without warning in the most well traveled channel. Water levels fluctuated widely due to snow melt, rain or freeze-up. Fog, snow and sudden freeze-up in the fall all posed serious risks as well and were responsible for several accidents. Massive caribou migrations across the river could also cause long, unplanned delays.

Perhaps the greatest risk to paddlewheelers was fire. Ships were lost to fire both on the river and in shipyards. While underway, embers from the smoke stack frequently landed on the canvas-covered decks. Deck hands were responsible for keeping this canvas constantly wet to reduce this risk. Crews practiced fire drills regularly, but many ships were lost all the same.

Frequently, paddlewheelers were inadvertently beached on gravel and sand bars. The entire river has its share of sand bars, especially the lower river and at the river's mouth at the Bering Sea. Getting off a sand bar was usually back-breaking, time-consuming work. In most cases the paddlewheelers were winched or their crews tried to wash away the gravel with the ship's paddlewheel. Sometimes passengers and cargo had to be unloaded to lighten the ship's draft. In desperation, large spars were driven into the sand until the ship lifted off the obstacle. It wasn't uncommon for ships to take days to get underway after landing on a sandbar.

The "Yukoner" on fire on the riverfront of Dawson City. May 2, 1900.

Five Finger Rapids, downstream of Carmacks, was the most serious obstacle on the river. Here the river drops through five rocky channels or "fingers." Paddlewheelers

usually went through this canyon under power at about 18 miles per hour to maintain control. The waves and current in the canyon made steering difficult. Navigating to avoid submerged rocks and around an intimidating cliff at the bottom of the rapid was difficult. More than one ship lost control in Five Finger Rapids and spun into the rocky cliff wall causing extensive hull and superstructure damage. Eventually a channel was blasted and navigating Five Finger Rapids became much easier.

When paddlewheelers were damaged, crews made enough repairs to allow them to safely limp to the next shipyard. Accounts of broken ribbing and planking being repaired with mattresses, or even sacks of flour, were not uncommon. When ships were wrecked, they were quickly stripped of anything of value and their hulking frames left to the river.

Above: The "Victorian" churning through the treacherous Five Finger Rapids on the Yukon River north of Carmacks.

Opposite: The "Columbian" after a black powder explosion and fire occurred at Eagle Rock on the Yukon River. The "Columbian" was carrying 3 tons of blasting powder for the Tantalus coal mine. A deckhand accidently tripped while shooting ducks and shot into the black powder which was stored in large corrugated iron kegs. The explosion killed six men and was the worst paddlewheeler disaster on the Yukon River. Fortunately the "Columbian" was only carrying 25 crew and no passengers due to the dangerous nature of the cargo. September 25, 1906.

They (victims of the "Columbian" explosion)...had every stitch of clothing (except their boots) blown off their bodies, which were burnt and charred and singed and blackened so as to hardly appear human, but they were not only alive but conscious and able to jump ashore when the captain rammed the bow into the bank and gave them the chance to jump.
S.H. Graves, 1908

Opposite Top: The "Klondyke"
partially submerged in the ice of
the Stewart River at Mayo, Yukon.
ca. 1924-25.

Opposite Bottom: The twisted
remains of the "James Domville"
minus the wheelhouse and smoke-
stack after sinking in the 30 Mile
section of the Yukon River.
Spring 1899.

Above: The "Yukoner" on fire at
Dawson City. May 2, 1900.

Pages 100 and 101: A view from
the deck of a paddlewheeler as it
navigates Five Finger Rapids. The
challenge was to avoid running into
the rocky outcrop in the middle of
the channel. To maintain control
Paddlewheelers had to travel faster
than the speed of the river and as a
result most ships traveled this rapid
at more than 18 miles per hour.

Happening within a month's time of the wreck of SS
Klondike, the Casca disaster is a severe blow to the Yukon
and a terrible blow to the British Yukon Navigation Company.
Faced with the encouraging prospects of one of its busiest
seasons in years, the loss of the Company's crack steamers is
indeed a catastrophe. An occasional wreck on the treacherous
Yukon River can easily be expected and the loss written off
but a series of major accidents such as the B.Y.N. Co. has
suffered this season, can only be ascribed to the worst kind of
luck and fate. All their season's operations have been disrupted
and held up as a result.
Mayo Miner, 10 July 1936

We left Whitehorse 7 PM on Wednesday night. It was just about noon as we steamed thru Five Finger rapids and as we were all on deck watching the sights. We were just on the way into the dining room when the Casca struck a rock about 300 yards past the old Dawson hull in Rink Rapids. The ship swung around and began to settle. It caught on the rock and hung there as the water rushed in the hull. Boats were put out and the passengers taken off at once. The boat is tilted somewhat on its side and is in 10 to 15 feet of water. The water at the spot where the wreck occurred is swift and we had quite a job shoving off in the small boats enroute to Yukon Crossing.
Mrs. Wm. Sime, 10 July 1936

Above: The "Dawson" navigating Five Finger Rapids. ca. 1905.

Opposite: The "Yukoner" going south through Five Finger Rapids. ca. 1900-1902.

DECLINE

In many ways the decline of the "golden age" of paddle-wheelers immediately followed the Klondike Gold Rush. The population of the region had mushroomed during the Gold Rush and collapsed soon afterward. In its heyday, in 1898, the Yukon had a population of more than 40,000 residents.

Many communities on the Yukon River went through bust and boom cycles as well. The White Pass and Yukon Route Railway had dire effects on settlements on the lower Yukon particularly St. Michael. The Great Depression of 1929 and the two World Wars also had dire effects on the economies of Alaska and the Yukon.

The sinking of the SS "Princess Sophia" near Juneau in 1918 cost more than 350 lives and deeply affected the region especially Circle and Dawson City where many of the passengers had lived. The "Sophia" was carrying a cross-section of northern society including many experienced paddlewheeler crew. At the time it was common for many residents to leave the north for the winter. In many ways, the communities along the Yukon River were more affected by the Sophia disaster than by almost any other factor. It would take decades for these towns to recover and rebound from this loss.

The depopulation of the Klondike region and the White Pass trade monopoly beached many paddle-wheelers in the decade following the Gold Rush. As each year passed, fewer and fewer paddlewheelers were required as the economic base was unable to support many ships. New transportation corridors were being established, most significantly was the construction of the Alaska Railway in 1923 which linked Valdez, Fairbanks and Nenana. The Alaska Railway reorganized trade on the lower Yukon River and made St. Michael little more than a name on a map.

The great paddlewheelers which once jockeyed for berths along the Dawson City waterfront gradually became less common and by the 1950s there were no working paddlewheelers on the upper Yukon River.

In addition, commercial airlines and bush planes started servicing the north. The final nail in the coffin was the completion of the Alaska Highway in 1942 and the extension of the Klondike Highway from Whitehorse to

Dawson shortly thereafter. The remaining paddlewheel-ers were put into service carrying supplies and US Army personnel to complete an undertaking which would lead to their end. By 1953 there were only a few working paddlewheelers, and these ships would soon be converted to cruise service and eventually become museum pieces. In total more than 250 paddlewheelers had served on the Yukon River. Only a few remain. The era of the great paddlewheelers on the Yukon River was over.

Above: Like most paddlewheelers the "Julia B.," "Seattle No. 3," "Schwatka" and an unidentified barge were left in dry dock to rot, be scavenged or burned. The few remains of these ships can be seen near the Dawson City Campground today.

Opposite: US army trucks being loaded onto barges to be towed on the Yukon River. Paddlewheelers carried army personnel as well as much needed supplies and equipment during the construction of the Alaska Highway.

Pages 108 and 109: The "Klondike"was the last active paddlewheeler on the Yukon River. When it was officially retired in 1968, the "Klondike" was moved along First Avenue in to its present location on the Whitehorse-waterfront.

Photograph Credits

This book is largely the result of the excellent care and preservation of images a hundred years old. Collections at the Yukon Archives, Whitehorse were used extensively.

Yukon Archives
Whitehorse, Yukon
Front Cover(2247), 4 (A-7417), 7 Bottom (736), 8 (5138), 10 (2314), 11 Top (3626), 11 Bottom (1196), 12 (1391), 13 Bottom (2120), 14/15 (3577), 16 (813), 18 Top (1557), 18 Bottom (2971), 19 (499), 20 (20), 21 (3319), 22/23 (6050), 24 (2255), 25 (4002), 26 (5167), 27 (2245), 28 (6641), 30 (8498), 31 (240), 32/33 (243), 34 Top (710), 34 Bottom (2079), 35 (4001), 36 (3609), 37 Top (3806), 37 Bottom (2085), 38/39 (8513), 40 (478), 41 (2241), 42 (2695), 43 Top (4004), 43 Bottom (6281), 44/45 (2247), 46 Top (833), 46 Bottom (2435), 47 (237), 48 (4623), 50 (4059), 51 Top (6639), 51 Bottom (4010), 52 (8501), 53 Top (6080), 53 Bottom (247), 54 (8501), 55 Top (4057), 55 Bottom (4003), 56 (5199), 58 Top (5204), 58 Bottom (5200), 59 (2693), 60 (5201), 63 (5523), 64 (5346), 65 Top (5519), 65 Bottom (5341), 66/67 (2711), 68 (3586), 69 (2739), 70/71 (3576), 72 (3178), 73 Top (5652), 73 Bottom (5551), 74 (3316), 75 Top (5548), 75 Bottom (4102), 76 (4008), 77 Top (5550), 77 Bottom (6031), 78 (2240), 78 (4006), 79 (4044), 80 (2249), 82 (3170), 83 Top (4105), 83 Bottom (3575), 84 (9409), 85 (711), 86/87 (5645), 88 Top (3990), 88 Bottom (5917), 89 (3992), 90/91 (3849), 92 (2245), 93 Top (4338), 93 Bottom (4000), 94 (2086), 96 (2140), 97 (5644), 98 Top (6717), 98 Bottom (4541), 99 (2447), 100/101 (4741), 102 (4018), 103 (2258), 104 (8511), 106 (7405), 107 (1949), 108/109 (2247), 110 (4011A), 112 (5643)

Alaska State Library,
Juneau
6 (PCA 4-60), 7 Top (PCA 87-83),

Alaska and Polar
Regions Department,
University of Alaska
Fairbanks
13 Top (#58-1026-153)

About the Author

Graham Wilson has lived in the north for more than a decade. He is the author of several books including *The Klondike Gold Rush: Photographs from 1896-1899*, *The White Pass and Yukon Route Railway*, and *Southeast Alaska: Early Photographs of the Great Land*. Graham is keenly interested in historic photographs and the stories that they tell.